MORE FOR 101 CLUES TO A HAPPY LIFE:

"Alex Bäcker has written this book that has become something of a phenomenon for everybody, not just for the kids... Really worthwhile tips that can change a life in a very practical way."

—Adriene Berg,
Emmy-winning host of Generation Bold:
The Fountain of Truth about Aging.

"Part Tim Ferris and part Kahlil Gibran, polymath renaissance man Alex Backer has distilled his advice for a happy life to 101 clues that, if investigated, may help you avoid some of the pitfalls in life. The genesis for this book was to impart some of the lessons that he has learned in life to his three children. Many of the clues are supplemented with humorous cartoons that drive the point home. Some of the clues are timeless while others reflect our modern times. Although the book is a quick read, each clue provides an opportunity to reflect upon the assumptions and priorities that for the basis of how we live our lives."

—Prof. Gino Yu,
Professor and Director of Digital Entertainment and Game Development, School of Design, Hong Kong Polytechnic University

101 Clues to a Happy Life

101 CLUES TO
A HAPPY LIFE

BY ALEX BÄCKER, PH.D.

MILL CITY PRESS

Mill City Press, Inc.
2301 Lucien Way #415
Maitland, FL 32751
407.339.4217
www.millcitypress.net

© 2022 by Alex Bäcker, Ph.D.

Alex Bäcker
alex@101clues.com

cartoonstock.com

Image on the preceding page courtesy Andrey Armyagov/ Shutterstock.com

All rights reserved solely by the author. The author guarantees all contents are original and do not infringe upon the legal rights of any other person or work. No part of this book may be reproduced in any form without the permission of the author.

Due to the changing nature of the Internet, if there are any web addresses, links, or URLs included in this manuscript, these may have been altered and may no longer be accessible. The views and opinions shared in this book belong solely to the author and do not necessarily reflect those of the publisher. The publisher therefore disclaims responsibility for the views or opinions expressed within the work.

Paperback ISBN-13: 978-1-6628-4218-4
Audiobook ISBN-13: 978-1-6628-4222-1
Ebook ISBN-13: 978-1-6628-4221-4

Dedicated to my children.

May you always preserve
your zest for life,
your kind heart,
your curiosity,
your passion,
your love for each other
and your happiness.

PREFACE

Life is a wonderful adventure. If only it came with a guide so we could avoid the mistakes made by others before us. This is my attempt at giving you that.

I started writing this book for my children in case I did not survive my planned expedition to Africa. I wanted to pass on much of what I would have taught them over the following years. It's been five years, and I have yet to carry out my Jeep expedition from Cairo to Cape Town. Yet, my oldest son is eighteen, and my daughter is twenty-one, so this seemed as good a time as any to pass on a few of the bits of insight I have acquired over the years, much of which I wish I had known earlier. After I wrote them, Steve Harrison, who has spent his professional life in the book industry, suggested they would be helpful to more than just my children.

So, here they are. I hope some of these turn out to be handy for you and your children. In this book, you will discover:

- How to get paid to travel the world
- How to get out of traffic tickets

- How to choose your mate and go after love
- How to recover from a fight with a loved one
- How to pick a career
- How to navigate a divorce (if you must)
- How to select a partner, a lawyer, or a home
- How to avoid the number one turn-off for people around you
- How to deal with jealousy and with fear
- How to get anyone's attention
- Why to dump toilet paper
- What is better to say than, "I'm sorry"
- When to go to sleep
- And much more.

These clues can make you a better lover, a better parent, a better leader and a better son or daughter. They will help you give memorable gifts. They will draw a lesson from The Beatles' enduring success toward your own. They will teach you how to prioritize.

I don't believe in fluff, so each clue is brief because I believe most ideas can be communicated rather concisely. As Mark Twain wrote, "I would have written you a shorter letter, but I ran out of time." Or as we say in Spanish, *"lo bue, si bre, dos ve bue,"* which translates to, "the good, if brief, twice as good."

I have tried to ensure they are not too brief. When I left for college, almost three decades ago, my mother gave me a copy of H. Jackson Brown's *Life's Little Instruction Book*. It was a fabulous book, which inspired me to write this one. Yet, for example, its instruction #93 says that ninety percent of all your happiness or misery will come from the life mate you choose—a decision it does not explain how to make. In brief, while I loved it, Life's Little Instruction Book is a little too little in some parts. I have striven to go a bit deeper, especially for some of those crucial clues – for example I have a whole clue devoted to how to pick a mate. Also, every person is different, which is why I have called these clues rather than instructions – you may find some clues you disagree with, and that's OK.

Americans are the unhappiest they've been in 50 years, a poll conducted by NORC at the University of Chicago found. Just 14% of U.S. adults say they're very happy. The proportion who say they are not too happy is the highest percentage on record since 1972. A record 4.5 million Americans quit their jobs last November. If you are one of the 86% of people who are not very happy, this book may help.

Fair would be to ask what qualifications I have to write a book like this. I have made many mistakes and have failed just as much as the next guy. So why did I write this book?

First, it is precisely *because* I have failed repeatedly that I have learned a few clues about life. I have been fired. I have lost most everything I owned. I have lost love. My ideas have been rejected too many times to count before they gained acceptance. In fact, I have learned so much about mistakes that I am writing an entire series of books about blunders you can't afford to make.

Second, I have had a few successes along the way (see my bio in the back of the book for details).

Third, despite my faults and peaks and valleys, I have lived an overall extremely happy life. In fact, when my mother blessed me by writing a book about my life on my 40th birthday, she titled it "Life is Wow", and put a photo of me with my typical face of *joie de vivre*, or "joy of life," on the cover.

Fourth, I have helped raise three happy children who are already showing they are winning at life. My oldest triple-majored in college in math, computer science, and history with a Trustee Fellowship, interned during college at NASA and the Federal Reserve, won an award at Harvard for her research on the influence of American Middle East policy on Anti-American sentiment and terrorist attacks, interviewed Wolf Blitzer and most presidential candidates as a student journalist, and before she finished college, had job offers from Princeton and Obama's former Chief Economist. My middle one represented his school at the Robotics World Championship, just started at Caltech (which is consistently ranked one of the top schools in the world), and is an accomplished pianist, bassist, runner, and mountain biker. My youngest son scored the first goal in the winning final that won his team the championship in one of AYSO's largest regions in the nation, has won top spots in long-distance races, and his team, for which he is both the pilot and one of the hardware and software engineers, currently leads the Southern California robotics league. They consistently tell me they are happy. And yet, they still make many of the same mistakes I made before them.

Enjoy the book. Most of all, enjoy this incredible life and the opportunities we are given. There may be 101 clues to living a happy life, but each of us gets only one life.

—Alex Bäcker,
Altadena, California,
February 1st, 2022

ACKNOWLEDGEMENTS

I am indebted to my parents, Ricardo Bäcker and Silvia Moos, for helpful comments on an earlier draft of this manuscript, including expanding some of the clues. To my mother, for gifting me my own little book of instructions when I first moved to a faraway land, which inspired me to write my own for my children. To Chel Hill for her generosity with her talent for cover design and the safe sex cartoon. To Chel Hill, Cindy Priscila and my editor MacKenzie Curry, for reviewing the manuscript and making it better. To Katya Gratcheva, for reminding me of one of the clues, to Kevin Manning, for the cover idea, and to Steve Harrison, for suggesting I publish this book.

TABLE OF CONTENTS

Preface xi
Acknowledgements xvii

1. On Family 1
2. How To Treat Your Mate 2
3. How To Pick A Lawyer 3
4. Pick Your Business Partners Carefully 4
5. How To Comfort A Mate 5
6. Make Your Life A Song 6
7. Be Kind Rather Than Right 7
8. Do Something You Love For A Living 8
9. If You Must Divorce, Do It Kindly 9
10. On Children 10
11. Don't Fall In Love, Dive In 11
12. Live Your Life In Color 12
13. Not All Wines Are Born Equal 13
14. The Pain Of Bread That's Not Pain 14
15. Buy The Best House You Can Afford 15
16. On Choosing A Mate 16
17. On Error-Correction, And De-Escalation 17
18. Take Everyone's Perspective In 18
19. Follow The Sun 19
20. Have As Many Passports As A Secret Agent . 20
21. Learn from Dr. Dolittle .21
22. Underpromise And Overdeliver 22
23. How To Avoid The Number One Turn-Off
    For People Around You 23

24. Dumping Toilet Paper 24
25. Make It Rain. 25
26. Keep Your Promises 26
27. On The Power Of Conversations With
    Your Children. 27
28. The Truth About Truth 28
29. Leave Your Mark. 29
30. On Massage. 30
31. Practice Mindfulness 31
32. Fear Is A Liar 32
33. Don't Jump From A Goldfish's Mouth
    Into A Shark's 33
34. Never Waste A Perfectly Good Opportunity
    To Celebrate. 34
35. On Live Music, Opera, and Musicals 35
36. Never Assume It's A Bad Idea Because
    It's Never Been Done. 36
37. On Video Games And Gambling. 37
38. Learn To Make Love Like Your Life
    Depended On It. 38
39. Drink Plenty Of Water 39
40. Start, And Then Keep Going 40
41. On Dancing 41
42. Invest In Books And Education 43
43. On Singing 43
44. On Exercise And Sports 44
45. On Coaching 45
46. Gadgets And Technology 46
47. On News. 47
48. How To Get Out Of A Ticket 48
49. How To Survive An Encounter With
    The Police. 49

XX — ALEX BÄCKER, PH.D.

50. On Jealousy In Relationships 51
51. On Safe Sex 51
52. On Trust 52
53. On Redundancy 53
54. On Plants 54
55. On Words. 55
56. On Complaining 56
57. On The Time To Go To Sleep 57
58. On How To Balance Conflicting Reasons
    To Do Opposite Things. 58
59. On Travel 59
60. On Hiring 60
61. On How To Get Insights. 61
62. On Getting People To Listen. 62
63. Swim. 63
64. On Toxic People 64
65. On Going After Love 65
66. On Elders 66
67. Don't Take It Personally. 67
68. Beware Projection 68
69. The Law of Diminishing Returns 69
70. Never Be Afraid To Say "I'm Sorry". 70
71. On Love After A Relationship. 71
72. A Relationship Is Worth More Than
    Most Issues 72
73. On Rest And Recreation 73
74. On Investing 74
75. Find Your Team 75
76. How To Get Anyone's Attention 76
77. Publish Or Perish. 78
78. Align Incentives. 79
79. Never Waste A Chance To Help 80

101 CLUES TO A HAPPY LIFE — XXI

80. Always Be There For Your Children and Your Partner 81

81. Dress Well 82

82. Find A Great Stylist....................... 83

83. Learn To Cook........................... 84

84. Watch The Sunset With Your Dog 85

85. Live Someplace Where You Can Hear Birds Singing 86

86. On How To Prioritize 87

87. Learn To Sail............................ 88

88. When Someone Shows You Who They Are, Believe Them............................ 89

89. Listen To Advice From Those More Experienced, But Trust Your Instincts....... 90

90. On The Power Of Self-Criticism 91

91. How To Travel The World For Free 92

92. On The Power Of Questions And Letting People Realize Things On Their Own 93

93. Don't Take No's As Final 94

94. How To Lead 95

95. Make Sure You Are Not Deficient In Key Vitamins 96

96. Keep Your Car And House Well Maintained.. 97

97. Leave Good Enough Alone 98

98. Nurture Your Relationships 99

99. Call Your Parents......................... 100

100. How To Give Great Gifts................... 101

101. Be Thankful.............................102

Further Resources 103

About The Author...........................104

1.
ON FAMILY

Stay close to it. Always. Nothing is more important. Nobody will love you as unconditionally.

"I guess we'd be considered a family. We're living together, we love each other, and we haven't eaten the children yet."

2.
HOW TO TREAT YOUR MATE

Make them feel loved, respected, and at peace. Make them feel good about themselves.

"That's the dating guru."

3.
HOW TO PICK A LAWYER

Don't save money on lawyers. You get what you pay for. Good lawyers know the law. Great lawyers know the judge, and they know how to tell the story. Judges will find a way to rule for who they believe to be the good guy.

Also, remember that lawyers and bankers work for *you*. You are the boss and the person who knows your situation best.

101 CLUES TO A HAPPY LIFE — 3

4.
PICK YOUR BUSINESS PARTNERS CAREFULLY

Reference-check potential partners. Reference-check their partners. Work with them for a test run before deciding to partner with them for good.

5.

HOW TO COMFORT A MATE

Hold them. Tell them that you love them. Listen to them. Make love to them. If they're really upset at you, there are two options that can work like magic:

1. Tell them, verbatim: "I am sorry I failed to make you feel like I was there for you when you needed me [or whatever it is you failed to do]. I will try harder and get better."

2. Tell them why you love them. Tell them everything you like about them.

These can get someone to go from not talking to you to telling you "I love you so much" in the blink of an eye.

6.

MAKE YOUR LIFE A SONG

Play music everywhere, most of the time. Curate a playlist for your life. Discover French music. Czech folk music. Jewish music. Spanish music. Mexican. Argentinian. 80s. Classic rock. German pop. Rap. Classical. The Beatles. Church music. Jazz.

Never stop discovering. Allow others to introduce you to what they love -in case you discover something you love, too. Don't worry about snobs who despise music that is commercial. Love what you love. If you have a chance to, write and record a song. When you do, collaborate with the best singers and producer(s) you can muster.

6 — ALEX BÄCKER, PH.D.

7.
BE KIND RATHER THAN RIGHT

Ending an argument is more important than winning it. Conversations are a way to design a better future.

Make the other party feel understood, even if you don't agree with them. Let them arrive at the right conclusion on their own.

"He's right, but he didn't have to rub our faces in it."

8.

DO SOMETHING YOU LOVE FOR A LIVING

We spend much of our lives working. Make sure you enjoy your work. Do something you will both be good at and have a good time doing. Learn what the daily life is like in any career you are considering, and choose something you love to do, not just something you like to learn about. A Myers-Briggs Type Indicator and a Harrison Assessment, which can give you a match score to any given profession, can help; make sure to take one of each early in your life.

9.

IF YOU MUST DIVORCE, DO IT KINDLY

I have experienced nothing more stressful than divorce, but remember that there is light at the end of the tunnel. A life full of love is more important than a life-long love. If you must divorce, write up agreements as soon as possible, while interests are aligned, and give it at least several months of an earnest last try where you are both trying to save the relationship.

10.
ON CHILDREN

If possible, have them. There is a love you won't experience until you do.

"It's a baby. Federal regulations prohibit our mentioning its race, age, or gender."

11.

DON'T FALL IN LOVE, DIVE IN

Love. Deeply. Don't be afraid to be hurt; fall in love hard. Tell your love how much you love them. Often. Don't settle for someone who doesn't love you the way you want to be loved. Love is the very best life has to offer us. Treasure it. Don't take it for granted. Fight for it.

12.
LIVE YOUR LIFE IN COLOR

Colors can produce happiness. Allow yourself that simple pleasure.

"Why on earth would you spring for color film?"

13.
NOT ALL WINES ARE BORN EQUAL

Malbec should be from Argentina or Chile. Shiraz should be from Australia or New Zealand. The quality of different wines is very different. Experience them and find out what you love. Keep track of them. I use an app called Delectable that will give you ratings by other users and even professionals for most any wine label you provide a photo of.

"What wine goes best with vodka?"

14.
THE PAIN OF BREAD THAT'S NOT *PAIN*

Look for restaurants with good bread. As a general principle, trust the French when it comes to bread.

15.
BUY THE BEST HOUSE YOU CAN AFFORD

As my Dad says, buy the best one you can afford. It's the best place to invest your money. You live your life in it.

16.

ON CHOOSING A MATE

This will be the most important decision of your life. Choose a mate who makes you their top priority. One you admire and find attractive. One who loves you. One who's wise and has a good heart. One who de-escalates conflict. One who treats children and animals well. One who loves music and enjoys your song, no matter its "quality." One who gives you peace and enjoys a good meal. One who loves to make love to you, but who also simply loves to just cuddle with you. One who laughs at your jokes and likes being touched by you. One who appreciates what you value. One who tells you that they love you. One who supports you and encourages you in your pursuits and makes you a better person. One whose smile you love. Chemistry is important. If they are the one, you will know pretty fast. Myers Briggs can be quite helpful in figuring out compatibility between personalities.

17.
ON ERROR-CORRECTION, AND DE-ESCALATION

99 percent of conflict is due to miscommunication. Verify that the message has not been lost in translation. This applies to your understanding too. De-escalate conflict. Humor is invaluable. Practice it constantly. Don't say hurtful things while you are hurt.

18.

TAKE EVERYONE'S PERSPECTIVE IN

There are multiple vantage points to any situation. A great solution can be derailed by failing to accommodate one key stakeholder. A leader takes all perspectives into account. This will enrich you and strengthen your relationships. It's not enough to listen. Make sure they *feel* heard. Show them you understand. Find compromise or devise a win-win solution. Life is short. If you can, spend it loving and building, not fighting, but don't shy away from a fight when it's the only way to get justice.

19.

FOLLOW THE SUN

Have a house with lots of sunlight. Spend as much time as you can outdoors.

20.
HAVE AS MANY PASSPORTS AS A SECRET AGENT

Get as many (nationalities) as you can. You never know when one will be handy.

"I'm a simple man really beneath the code words and the black ops and the multitude of fake passports."

21.
LEARN FROM DR. DOLITTLE

If practical, get one or more pets. Nobody will show you as much gratitude or appreciation.

"And then I just hit delete. I haven't actually eaten any homework in years."

22.
UNDERPROMISE AND OVERDELIVER

Perception, and thus satisfaction, has more to do with expectations than with performance. Make sure to underpromise and overdeliver.

"Worst-case scenario? The renovation goes three years and two million dollars over budget, one of you bludgeons me to death with my own hammer, and you both get the electric chair."

23.
HOW TO AVOID THE NUMBER ONE TURN-OFF FOR PEOPLE AROUND YOU

To prevent bad breath, brush your teeth after every meal, floss often, and use a Listerine mouthwash every morning, especially as you get older. Brush your tongue.

101 CLUES TO A HAPPY LIFE — 23

24.
DUMPING TOILET PAPER

Toilet paper is obsolete. Get a toilet that allows you to wash your behind – you can buy one for less than a family pack of toilet paper. If that fails, use moist towels. If you stepped on poop, would you clean your foot with toilet paper?

25.
MAKE IT RAIN

Take a shower or bath frequently –I like to take one every day. A Japanese study showed that people who bathe more frequently than three times per week exhibited a better physical and psychological state. Always take one before you go out on a date. Enjoy bubble baths and scented mineral salts.

26.

KEEP YOUR PROMISES

Don't make one you don't intend to keep. Your credibility is one of your most valuable assets.

27.

ON THE POWER OF CONVERSATIONS WITH YOUR CHILDREN

Answer questions as they get posed. Teach your children about their roots, and give them wings. Let them into your life; it will be a valuable source of lessons for them and will strengthen your bond. Pass on to them what you have learned, whether you write your own book or gift them a book like this one.

28.
THE TRUTH ABOUT TRUTH

Never lie. Trust is hard to earn and easy to lose. But don't use honesty as an excuse to say hurtful things. If it causes more hurt than good, it may be best not said. Find the kindest way to tell the truth.

"Yes, I received your resume that you emailed. I ran a fact check and I was wondering if you know that a half truth is a whole lie."

29.

LEAVE YOUR MARK

At least once in your life, invent something unique that makes the world a better place. Get it built and used. Perhaps that means starting a company. Perhaps it means writing a book. Perhaps it means recording a song or making a movie. Teaching something that matters. Changing a process, perhaps by involving yourself in a government organization –for example, I have written about changes I would like to see in the way elections are run or in the way billing mistakes are handled. Whatever it is, never give up control of it unless you are ready to sell it. Nobody will care about it more or understand it better.

30.
ON MASSAGE

Touch is touching. Enjoy a massage. Find a good masseuse/masseur; they vary a lot. Enjoy aromatic candles, bath salts, hot stones, and aromatic massage oil too.

"Only way I could get him to come was to tell him it was massage therapy."

31.
PRACTICE MINDFULNESS

Practice mindfulness for at least ten minutes every morning to learn to live in the present moment. Do not take your thoughts and state of mind for granted, but rather as something temporary that will pass. Learn to perceive your state of mind so you are able to step outside of it and put it in perspective, if not control it.

DR. FLAGG'S WORST NIGHTMARE

32.
FEAR IS A LIAR

Fear is not a good guide for decision-making. First, when you are afraid, your neocortex (the part of your brain required for insights) shuts off. Second, most things we fear never come to happen. Third, fear won't prevent them from happening. Stay calm, worry only about things within your control, and navigate life for the best available outcome.

"Well, now that you have it, you can stop worrying about getting it."

32 — ALEX BÄCKER, PH.D.

33.

DON'T JUMP FROM A GOLDFISH'S MOUTH INTO A SHARK'S

Don't assume that because something is bad it cannot get worse. Things can always get worse. Don't change for the sake of change; be thoughtful about all alternatives.

34.
NEVER WASTE A PERFECTLY GOOD OPPORTUNITY TO CELEBRATE

Celebrate Christmas, birthdays, St. Patrick's Day, and every good opportunity to have a special day. Make it special for your children. No matter your religion or lack thereof. Enjoy the food and the music. As my mother once said in a graduation speech, traditions are valuable because of how they make us feel. Enjoy the *Vorfreude*—a marvelous German word to describe the joy of anticipation.

34 — ALEX BÄCKER, PH.D.

35.
ON LIVE MUSIC, OPERA, AND MUSICALS

Yes. Go see the music you love with someone you love. Listening to a live instrument is better than a recording. Seeing the musicians play brings the music to life. But it's also about the experience, about putting a face to the music you love, and about the memories you will create.

101 CLUES TO A HAPPY LIFE — 35

36.

NEVER ASSUME IT'S A BAD IDEA BECAUSE IT'S NEVER BEEN DONE

Never tell yourself that if it was any good, it would have been done before. If everybody told themselves that, no progress would ever have been made.

36 — ALEX BÄCKER, PH.D.

37.
ON VIDEO GAMES AND GAMBLING

Everything in moderation.

"I can't play video games with you after school. I have to help my father help me with my homework."

38.
LEARN TO MAKE LOVE LIKE YOUR LIFE DEPENDED ON IT

Some things you just can't get too much of. Biology self-regulates your need for sex. If you can have it and want to, you probably shouldn't feel bad about having it. Sex makes everything better. Focus on the other person, and everything else will follow.

"Now that the kids are grown and gone, I thought it might be a good time for us to have sex."

39.
DRINK PLENTY OF WATER

Lots of it. It helps prevent kidney stones, among other things. It helps your skin. We evolved from sea creatures, where we were constantly bathed by water, and the closer we stay to that, the happier our bodies are.

"How is the water prepared?"

40.

START, AND THEN KEEP GOING

"Create the grandest possible vision for your life, because you become what you believe."
—Oprah Winfrey

"Whether you think you can or you think you can't, you are right."
—Henry Ford

"Life is trying things to see if they work."
—Ray Bradbury

"The secret to getting ahead is getting started."
—Mark Twain

"Don't wait. The time will never be just right."
—Napoleon Hill

"It doesn't matter how slow you go as long as you do not stop."
—Confucius

41.
ON DANCING

Learn to dance the tango with an Argentinian teacher. Waltz in Vienna. Watch a ballet at the Bolshoi in Moscow. Dance like nobody is watching. Dancing is about two things and two things alone: enjoying the music and connecting with your partner. Let the music lead you.

"Mummy, all the ballerinas were on tiptoe. Why don't they just use taller dancers?"

42.

INVEST IN BOOKS AND EDUCATION

Books can take you to faraway lands, to long-gone times, and into other people's minds. Buy one anytime you feel like it. My mother taught me to feel good about spending on books. Build a library you cherish. And at least once in your life, write a book.

There is no better investment than in making you and your children wiser and better people.

43.
ON SINGING

Singing feeds the soul. Just do it. Especially in the shower. Build a shower with tiles that make your singing reverberate. Sing at karaoke. Sing like nobody is listening.

"I don't sing because I am happy. I am happy because I sing."

44.

ON EXERCISE AND SPORTS

Sports are better than exercise; they combine exercise, a goal, competition, and often teamwork. Play a sport you like, and compete like you care. You don't need to be good at a sport in order to enjoy it. If you prefer to run or bike, try to run or bike in a place you love. Enjoy the wind in your face. Enjoy the changing views. At a minimum, walk your dog twice a day.

45.
ON COACHING

It's your second chance at a sporting career or any hobby. It's a chance for a cerebral person to be good at sports. Care about it. Put passion into it or don't do it (this applies to everything).

"I told him to do that."

46.

GADGETS AND TECHNOLOGY

Keep a locator with your wallet, keys, and passport—gone are the days when my Caltech classmates and I schemed about inventing something like that; you can buy one for a few bucks. Carry an extra battery for your phone. Schedule emails so they go out an hour after you write them—the following morning for important ones. Your brain will keep processing them in the background and will often keep coming up with improvements. Once an hour passes without you wanting to make any changes to your email, it's ready to go out. Use Pandora to discover music. Own a great music system.

47.
ON NEWS

Read the news. You are lucky to watch history unfold before your eyes. Many interesting events will happen in your lifetime. At least once in your life, be the news. In a good way.

"And, while there's no reason yet to panic, I think it only prudent that we make preparations to panic."

48.
HOW TO GET OUT OF A TICKET

If you get pulled over by a law enforcement officer for an infraction, try asking them: "Do you have the power to forgive me?" You'll be amazed at what the desire to appear powerful will do.

49.
HOW TO SURVIVE AN ENCOUNTER WITH THE POLICE

If you get pulled over or stopped by a police officer, do not move your hands unless the officer tells you to. When you do, do it slowly and always within view of the police officer. Remember that they don't know you and work around dangerous people, so an innocent move can look like a sign of danger to them.

"Do I know how fast I was going? Isn't that your job?"

50.
ON JEALOUSY IN RELATIONSHIPS

Learn to embrace the fact that being jealous of someone means that you love them. Remove that word from your vocabulary. Find a partner who feels the same. Honor that trust by always prioritizing the person you love.

"I hope you kept the box it came in."

51.
ON SAFE SEX

You are descended from a very fertile lineage: every single one of your ancestors got pregnant or left someone pregnant. STDs can be fatal or last forever. Practice safe sex until you find the person you love. Always carry condoms.

SAFE SEX

52.

ON TRUST

Trust the person you love, and be trustworthy. Trust requires interaction, disclosure, and flexibility. In work, trust but verify.

53.
ON REDUNDANCY

Create redundancy in your organization as soon as you can so you are not overly dependent on any one person. Keep spare keys, spare cash, and a spare credit card outside your wallet.

"At this point, I'm just happy to still have a job."

101 CLUES TO A HAPPY LIFE — 53

54.
ON PLANTS

Surround yourself with them—just don't forget to water them.

"I can tell it's new because it's alive."

54 — ALEX BÄCKER, PH.D.

55.

ON WORDS

Be careful with them. They can hurt. Think before you talk. Often, silence can be the best answer. As Winston Churchill said, "We are masters of the unsaid words, but slaves of those we let slip out". If you disagree with something said at a meeting, it may sometimes be more effective to ignore it than to debate it – the outcome of a meeting is more often determined by the direction the conversation takes than by anybody convincing anybody else. Also, pause after every point you make to get a reaction before moving on to your next one.

56.
ON COMPLAINING

Do as little of it as possible with the people you love. If the good outweighs the bad, take the good with the bad.

"Can I bring you something else to complain about?"

57.
ON THE TIME TO GO TO SLEEP

Go to bed with your partner as much as possible. You can always wake up early the next morning.

"Insomnia is very common. Try not to lose any sleep over it."

58.

ON HOW TO BALANCE CONFLICTING REASONS TO DO OPPOSITE THINGS

Complex decisions will often have different factors pointing in opposite directions. Weigh each appropriately, prioritizing what matters most.

"Yes, the planet got destroyed. But for a beautiful moment in time we created a lot of value for shareholders."

59.

ON TRAVEL

Do lots of it. Don't stay at chain hotels, experience local life. Travel allows you to briefly live life someone else's way. The mind thrives on change; it's the only thing we even perceive. Do enough planning to enjoy *Vorfreude* (the joy of anticipation) but leave enough freedom to allow for spontaneous detours. Read about the history of every place you visit. Learn a little of the language—a word or two in people's language can go a long way in getting you hospitality. As James Norbury said in response to the age-old question of whether it's the journey or the destination, it's the company.

60.
ON HIRING

Hire slow, and fire fast. Evaluate new hires after ninety days as if you were rehiring them. Fire disloyal or dishonest people without hesitation.

"It's OK, everyone makes mistakes. Look at me. I hired you."

61.
ON HOW TO GET INSIGHTS

Thought occurs at five different levels. At the top is vision for desired outcomes. Below that are plans. Beneath those are details. Then are problems. At the bottom is drama. Live your life in the top three levels. When you are stuck in drama or feel threatened, your amygdala gets activated, and the prefrontal cortex, the part of the brain that is capable of insights, is suppressed. Emerge to think about the vision of where you want to be and enter a state of reward – feel good about yourself–, and insights will emerge.

"I'm just sitting here waiting for an idea who's time has come...but apparently it's running late."

62.
ON GETTING PEOPLE TO LISTEN

Make sure those you want to listen to you feel that you value their status, that they have some certainty of what's coming, that they feel the autonomy to make decisions, that they feel aligned with you, and that they feel fairly treated. If they don't, their amygdala will interfere.

"When you said we needed to talk, you didn't say I needed to listen."

63.
SWIM

Swimming exercises many of your muscles, cures back pain, and refreshes you. Consider a daily swim.

"This pool's no fun — All they let you do is swim."

64.
ON TOXIC PEOPLE

Disconnect them from your life. Your mood is affected by those around you. Your life is dictated by what you think, what you do, who you spend time with, and where you are, so be mindful about each.

"Let's not ruin this moment by enjoying it."

64 — ALEX BÄCKER, PH.D.

65.

ON GOING AFTER LOVE

Wait for a potential mate to notice you before you show them your interest; anticipation breeds desire. Don't be shy to show them how you feel; they want to be loved too. Don't be fazed by rejection. It's only temporary, and you can't lose what you don't have. There are 3.8 billion men and 3.8 billion women in the world; there is more than one who can make you happy. Find an opportunity to talk to them; you will become more attractive when they see your mind at work. Women like confidence; approach them like you know they will like you, and they likely will. Don't talk to a woman about another woman. The woman who will fall in love with you is typically one who orgasms with you. Learn to please her like it's your most valuable skill. Plan interesting dates. Show interest in their life. Learn to dance. You can get most anyone to be interested in you.

66.
ON ELDERS

Prioritize time with them, even if it's a short call or message that shows them that you care, lest they die before you get to them. The most inexorable of deadlines is death.

"Remember when self respect and respect for elders was two different things?"

67.
DON'T TAKE IT PERSONALLY

Most people's reactions to what you do have more to do with them than with you. Conversely, while you can't control how others treat you or everything that happens to you, you are 100 percent in control of how you react. As my Dad says, "If they didn't hurt you or they didn't mean to hurt you, there is nothing to be upset about."

68.

BEWARE PROJECTION

Most people tend to assume others think like they do themselves. This is the reason the golden rule is known as "Do unto others as you would like to have done unto you". Yet this is a terrible assumption. People are dramatically different from each other. The most human of all traits —although of course not unique to humans— is our neural plasticity, and that makes for huge diversity among humans.

Don't assume that others will react like you would have reacted yourself. Learn to predict how different people would react to the same situation. In fact, I suggest you write yourself a brief instruction manual for each key person in your life.

The right rule for how to treat people is: "Do unto others as they would like to be treated."

69.

THE LAW OF DIMINISHING RETURNS

Goods and experiences diminish their value to you as you get more of them. This means you can get most of the happiness you'd derive from any one by getting a little bit of it. The first night in a great hotel will mean much more than subsequent ones. The first week of vacation will mean more than the next ones. A little bit of enjoying a pleasant activity can get you much of the relaxation you'd get from carrying on. Variety is the spice of life. So when you are staying somewhere for a single night, splurge on your lodging, and when renting a car for a weekend, get one you love.

70.
NEVER BE AFRAID TO SAY "I'M SORRY"

To err is human. To apologize is divine—even when feelings have been hurt without you being at fault. Whenever possible, make your apologies in person – especially in matters of love. On the other hand, a "thank you" may be more effective than an apology. For example, "thank you for your patience" is better than "I'm sorry I'm late." Focus on the positive and the other person rather than the negative and you.

71.

ON LOVE AFTER A RELATIONSHIP

Stay on good terms with the people you have loved. Love does not have an off switch. You will only share your heart and life with so many people, and you will get peace from extending your loving feelings beyond the end of a relationship.

72.
A RELATIONSHIP IS WORTH MORE THAN MOST ISSUES

It's OK to make your viewpoint known, even if it's different than others'. But if and once you have made your viewpoint known and it has been rejected, consider whether the relationship involved is worth more than the particular point you are trying to press. Usually it is. If so, consider dropping your point in favor of the relationship.

73.
ON REST AND RECREATION

I have loved my career, and yet, as my father anticipated to me, my greatest joys have come from elsewhere. From love. From my children. From travel. From film and music. From creating. From delicious meals. So give yourself permission to relax and enjoy life any time you want to. The purpose of life is happiness.

"And remember, if you need anything I'm available 24/6."

101 Clues to a Happy Life — 73

74.
ON INVESTING

Cash only loses its value over time. The NASDAQ-100 Technology Sector Index has almost tripled in the last twenty years—even though there was a bubble twenty years ago. Unless you need the money in the next year or so, keep most of your savings invested most of the time. If you pick a diversified portfolio well, your fortune will grow as fast as that of the best entrepreneurs. If in doubt, invest in technology. It has been the main engine of economic progress. Look for algorithmic portfolio managers with a track record; investing is a task best done by machines due to the sheer amount of data involved.

"The little pig with the portfolio of straw and the little pig with the portfolio of sticks were swallowed up, but the little pig with the portfolio of bricks withstood the dip in the market."

75.

FIND YOUR TEAM

Work with people who have skills complementary to yours. You can't, and shouldn't, do everything yourself. Delegate. And when you find a good team, keep it. Take Paul McCartney, the most successful albums act in UK official chart history. He has had three UK singles for a total of eight weeks at number-one in over fifty years. John Lennon, his bandmate, had three number-one singles for a total of seven weeks in a decade as a soloist. Their "team," The Beatles, had seventeen UK hits for a total of sixty-five weeks at number-one in just one decade. In other words, The Beatles were 5-10 times more successful than their members were on their own. They failed to appreciate the role their team played in their success, and the world paid the price.

"So what can you bring to this partnership?"

101 CLUES TO A HAPPY LIFE — 75

76.
HOW TO GET ANYONE'S ATTENTION

You can get anyone to reply to you provided you personalize and time your missive right. Early Sunday mornings work better for busy overachievers. First establish an emotional connection. Everybody, no matter how successful, appreciates genuine admiration. Then show how you can add value to them, concisely. End with what you want to ask for.

101 Clues to a Happy Life — 77

77.

PUBLISH OR PERISH

Write or record your thoughts before you forget them. Publish them. The world belongs to those who publish their ideas, not those who only write them. Publish in a citable medium.

78.
ALIGN INCENTIVES

There are people who seek to win at the expense of others, and people who seek to create something where there was nothing before. Partner only with people with a win-win philosophy who seek to enlarge the cake rather than get a bigger fraction for themselves, and align incentives so you can all win together.

"So, it's agreed - we lay off the stick and hit them hard with the carrot."

79.
NEVER WASTE A CHANCE TO HELP

People rarely ask for help. When they do, go out of your way to drop everything you are doing and help. It is a gift to be able to help someone. A friend in need is a friend indeed.

"I *really* appreciate this..."

80.

ALWAYS BE THERE FOR YOUR CHILDREN AND YOUR PARTNER

My children are my top priority in life. Children who know their parents are always there for them grow up feeling safe and secure. Yet, children should not come at the expense of your life partner. Make room for both.

81.
DRESS WELL

Impressions matter. Perception matters. Dress to impress. It will make you look better and make you feel better too.

"Look at you! Breaking out the _good_ sweatpants today."

82.
FIND A GREAT STYLIST

You'd be amazed at what a difference a good haircut makes. All haircuts were not born equal, and neither were all stylists. Find one that knows how to give you a look you love.

83.
LEARN TO COOK

A delicious home-cooked meal can be the way to a man's heart, can make a house a home, and is a wonderful thing to share both with your loved one and with your children. Learn to cook at least one great meal, and make it with love.

84.

WATCH THE SUNSET WITH YOUR DOG

Sunsets are beautiful. Pause to watch each with your dog if you can—or rise in time to watch the sunrise. There is no better way to appreciate the passing of the seasons than to see how quickly the sunrise and sunset time change with the seasons.

85.
LIVE SOMEPLACE WHERE YOU CAN HEAR BIRDS SINGING

Birds' song makes people happier. It's a scientific fact. We have evolved to love nature. Find your corner of it.

"You're not going to put that there, are you?"

86.

ON HOW TO PRIORITIZE

I have long held Bäcker's Prioritization Paradox:

1. Prioritizing is difficult because you have to consider every possible task in doing so.

2. Prioritizing is easy because all you have to decide is what the most important or urgent task(s) is/are right now.

So consider everything, but only to the extent of figuring out which your top one, two, or three priorities are. Then, worry about nothing else. That will clear your mind and provide much needed focus.

I have found I can successfully tackle up to three priorities simultaneously—for example, I once financed my company, fought for time with my children, and bought a house at the same time. But that required dropping priorities four and beyond.

87.
LEARN TO SAIL

It's easy, and it's less expensive than you may think. It's relaxing to be in the sunlight, sense the wind in your face, and hear and see the water. It also makes for the best dates.

88.

WHEN SOMEONE SHOWS YOU WHO THEY ARE, BELIEVE THEM

When someone disappoints you, learn from it, and don't give them a chance to disappoint you again. This doesn't mean you shouldn't give people you love second chances, but it does mean you should not ignore the clues you pick up along the way.

89.

LISTEN TO ADVICE FROM THOSE MORE EXPERIENCED, BUT TRUST YOUR INSTINCTS

Experience helps. Yet nobody knows yourself and your circumstances better than you do.

90.

ON THE POWER OF SELF-CRITICISM

When dealing with someone who holds a negative opinion of you, disarm them by self-criticizing so extensively that they start defending you. You don't need to agree with their criticism. Just say "I know you think I ...". It works!

91.

HOW TO TRAVEL THE WORLD FOR FREE

Rent your house out on Airbnb, Vrbo, and Booking. com. Then use the proceeds to travel to your favorite destinations. If you live in a relatively expensive part of the world, such as the US or Europe, you can usually live in style in less expensive parts of the world and still have money left over to pay for your airfare and even make a profit. Invest in making your property stand out in a way that will make people want to spend a mini-vacation there.

92.

ON THE POWER OF QUESTIONS AND LETTING PEOPLE REALIZE THINGS ON THEIR OWN

Instead of telling people what to do, ask them questions that leads them to realize the way on their own. The mind values its own conclusions more highly than anybody else's.

93.

DON'T TAKE NO'S AS FINAL

I had bought a roundtrip ticket from the USA to the Seychelles, when the airline emailed me on the day of my departure asking me to call them for an important message about my flight. I called, and got put on hold. When the airline finally picked up, they told me that my return flight had gotten canceled. I had two options, they said: cancel my trip—30 minutes before I left for the airport and after I had already booked a nonrefundable week-long yacht cruise—, or pay $13,000 to change to a worse flight that had two long stopovers. I asked for a supervisor. He gave me the same options. I asked to talk to someone else, but he said there was nobody else to speak to then. I insisted for 90 minutes, and suddenly the $13,000 change fee vanished.

But I was still seemingly stuck with two long stopovers. When I got to my stopover in Zurich, I asked a Swiss airline employee about the flight that had allegedly been canceled. It turns out the flight had simply been moved back a few hours. She rebooked me on my original flight.

A no is just a yes that hasn't happened yet.

94.
HOW TO LEAD

Leaders are distinguished by how far into the future they see and how long they can go without coming back for instructions. Rote workers can only carry out a simple task before returning for instructions. Managers keep going for longer. Executives can create plans for an entire year. True leaders have the vision to create multi-year plans and keep coming up with new goals. Have the courage to be a leader. Be self-driven.

95.

MAKE SURE YOU ARE NOT DEFICIENT IN KEY VITAMINS

Hundreds of expert doctors and scientists recommend you supplement with at least 2,000 to 4,000 IU of vitamin D daily during the winter if you live far from the equator, to keep your vitamin D levels from being deficient. There is evidence it may help prevent a number of ailments, including COVID-19 (see vitaminDforall.org for details).

96.

KEEP YOUR CAR AND HOUSE WELL MAINTAINED

It's a slippery slope once you start letting it slip. By getting used to keeping them in great condition, repairs never pile up. Also, a repair need that goes unheeded for too long can cause additional damage. Best of all, you get to enjoy a house and a car in great shape.

97.
LEAVE GOOD ENOUGH ALONE

When an offer is good enough, consider accepting it without negotiation. The chances of reaching agreement go down significantly when you say no and counter. Time kills every deal.

"There's nothing wrong with the ship. We just got a better offer."

98.
NURTURE YOUR RELATIONSHIPS

Keep in touch with friends and acquaintances. Any time you meet someone or discover something you think would be helpful to someone you know, send it to them. Imagine the power of your entire network looking out for you rather than just yourself –it's a multiplicative effect. That's the gift you want to give your network. To this end, know what the people you know care about.

"I'm sorry, dear. I wasn't listening. Could you repeat what you've said since we've been married?"

99.
CALL YOUR PARENTS

Nobody will ever love you as unconditionally. Treasure your parents, keep them up to date on your life, and call or visit them at least once a week.

"O.K., Mom, I'm off the plane. I'll call you when I check into the hotel, and when I check out of the hotel, when I get on the plane home, and when I get off the plane home, and I'll call you when I'm in the driveway—glad you're not worrying."

100.
HOW TO GIVE GREAT GIFTS

Gift-giving is about the time and thought you put into it. It's about giving the recipient something they would not have known or thought to get themselves. That's why I never give money or any commodity. Put in the time to put a little bit of you into each of your gifts. Who do you know who could benefit from this book? Get them a copy today. Perhaps add some of your own clues, too. Wisdom is a wonderful thing. Pass it on.

101.
BE THANKFUL

You have lots to be thankful for. If you are reading this book, chances are you are luckier than most of the world. There are undoubtedly a large number of people in history who had it worse than you—in all probability, most people who ever lived. Don't forget it, and don't forget to thank those responsible for any of it. Be mindful that there will be a last time for everything you do, so enjoy every time. Thankfulness is an ingredient of happiness.

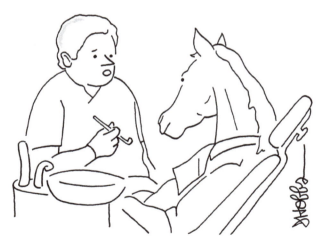

"You're not a gift horse, are you?"

FURTHER RESOURCES:

Life's Little Instruction Book by H. Jackson Brown's contains an excellent list of rules to live by.

The Success Principles: How To Get From Where You Are To Where You Want To Be, by Jack Canfield, is a superb detailed guidebook to success.

The How of Happiness, by Sonja Lyubomirsky, a science-based approach to achieving happiness.

The Happiness Lab Podcast by Laurie Santos: https://www.happinesslab.fm/

Additional 101 Clues resources are available at 101clues.com, where you can use the password MUSICMAKESMEHAPPY to unlock a free song I composed and recorded with chart-topping writer Chel Hill. Sign up for the 101 Clues newsletter there and like 101Clues on Facebook to be the first to be notified when new clues are released!

ABOUT THE AUTHOR

Alex Bäcker is a father of three. Recently, he (barely) survived having all three experience their teenage years at the same time. He has made or witnessed enough mistakes to write an entire series of books about them, which he is in the process of publishing.

He was National Olympic Champion of Informatics in his native Argentina when he was 18, went to college at MIT and Harvard, got a Ph.D. at the California Institute of Technology (Caltech), raised $10 million to become CEO of his first company three years out of grad school, and went on to found QLess, a company that saved hundreds of millions of waits, gave its users more time back than all of recorded history, and was crowned the "Best Small or Medium Computer Services Company in the USA" six consecutive years, earning him the title of "Best IT Executive of the Year" at the International Business Awards.

He was named one of the Top 100 MIT Technology Alumni and one of 40 under 40. He has given TEDx talks in two languages on two continents. Dr. Bäcker's work has been featured in *Time* magazine, the New York Times, the Wall Street Journal, TechCrunch, Huffpost Live, CNET, the BBC, *Fast Company*, *Entrepreneur*, NPR, Fox News, ABC, NBC and many other leading news outlets. He is the inventor behind eleven patents. His scientific discoveries have been published in leading journals, including *Nature and Neural Computation*. He was the discoverer of the preventative role of sunlight and vitamin D for COVID-19.

He has traveled to seventy-two countries and forty-nine US states. In his spare time, he composes music. He lives an unabashedly happy life.

CPSIA information can be obtained
at www.ICGtesting.com
Printed in the USA
BVHW021357180522
637331BV00023B/522